For all at Holy Family School,
Southampton
M.C.

For Carrie Rose
G.W.

First published in the United States 1998 by
LITTLE TIGER PRESS
N16 W23390 Stoneridge Drive, Waukesha, W1 53188
Originally published in Great Britain 1998 by Magi Publications
Text © 1998 Michael Coleman
Illustrations © 1998 Gwyneth Williamson
Library of Congress-Cataloging-in-Publication Data
Coleman, Michael, 1946 May 12–
One, two, three, oops! / by Michael Coleman ;
illustrated by Gwyneth Williamson.
p.   cm.   Summary : Mr. Rabbit becomes frustrated when he tries to count
his active, constantly moving babies and keeps having to start over.
ISBN 1-888444-45-2
[1. Rabbits--Fiction.   2. Babies--Fiction.   3. Counting--Fiction.]
I. Williamson, Gwyneth, 1965–   ill. II. Title
PZ7.C677160n   1998   [E]--dc21   98-6476 CIP AC

One, Two, Three, Oops!

by Michael Coleman
Pictures by Gwyneth Williamson

Mr. and Mrs. Rabbit had a big family . . .

A very big family . . .

A very, very big family!

"I wonder how many bunnies we have," said Mr. Rabbit one morning. "I think I'll count them today."

"Why not wait until later?" said Mrs. Rabbit. "I would."

"No," said Mr. Rabbit firmly. "I'll do it now."

He went outside to where the bunnies
were playing. Mr. Rabbit started counting.
"One, two, three—oops! Oh, noggin-sploggin!"
he exclaimed.

With a hop and a skip, the bunnies he'd been counting ran off to join their brothers and sisters. He couldn't tell which ones he'd counted and which ones he hadn't.

Mr. Rabbit started again. This time he got
a little further. "One, two, three, four—oops!
Oh, noggin-sploggin, boodle-doodle!" he
grumbled.

The bunnies had started a game
of tag, and he'd lost count again.

Mr. Rabbit tried one more time.
"One, two, three, four, five—oops!
Oh, noggin-sploggin, boodle-doodle,
grizzly-wizzly!" he groaned.

The bunnies had started playing hide-and-seek.
Now he couldn't see any of them, and he'd lost
count again.

"This is no good," said Mr. Rabbit. "I'll have to
think of a better way to count our bunnies."

So he sat and thought until he had a good idea. "I know," he said. "I'll give a carrot to every bunny I count. That way I'll see the ones I've missed." So Mr. Rabbit started counting again. This time he handed a carrot to each bunny he counted. "One, two, three, four, five, six—oops! Oh, noggin-sploggin, boodle-doodle, grizzly-wizzly, sniffy-whiffy!" he cried.

The bunnies
he'd given carrots
to had eaten them!
He couldn't tell
which ones he'd
counted and which
ones he hadn't.

Then Mr. Rabbit
had another good idea.
"I'll tell them to sit down
when I've counted them.
That way I won't get
mixed up."

So Mr. Rabbit told his bunnies to sit down once he'd counted them. "One, two, three, four, five, six, seven—oops! Oh, noggin-sploggin, boodle-doodle, grizzly-wizzly, sniffy-whiffy, jingle-bingle!" he shouted.

The ground was full of prickly weeds.
Just as soon as the bunnies sat down, they
jumped up again, and Mr. Rabbit had lost count
once more.

Mr. Rabbit thought and thought, and finally
he had another idea. "I will send every bunny
I count indoors. The ones still outside will be
the ones I haven't counted. I can't possibly get
mixed up that way!"

So Mr. Rabbit started counting again. This
time every bunny he counted was sent indoors.
"One, two, three, four, five, six, seven, eight—oops!
Oh, noggin-sploggin, boodle-doodle, grizzly-wizzly,
sniffy-whiffy, jingle-bingle, fuddle-duddle!" yelled
Mr. Rabbit, stamping his foot.

He'd forgotten that their home had
a back door. Every bunny he'd sent in
the front had come out the back way.
He'd lost count yet again.

Mr. Rabbit wouldn't give up. He sat down once more and thought all afternoon . . .

and all evening. Then he noticed a patch of mud on the ground and had his best idea yet.

"I've got it!" said Mr. Rabbit. "I'll put a dab of mud on the tail of every bunny I count. Then I'll know that the bunnies with clean tails are the ones I haven't counted. I can't possibly get mixed up that way."

So Mr. Rabbit began to count once more. Every time he counted a bunny, he put a blob of mud on its tail.

"One, two, three, four, five, six, seven, eight, nine—oops! Oh, noggin-sploggin, boodle-doodle, grizzly-wizzly, sniffy-whiffy, jingle-bingle, fuddle-duddle, jungle-bungle!" he roared, jumping up and down.

It had started to rain. All the blobs of mud he'd put on the bunnies had washed away. He'd lost count yet again!

"I give up!" said Mr. Rabbit. He stomped angrily back indoors. "I'll never be able to count all our bunnies!" he cried.

At that moment Mr. and Mrs. Rabbit's bunnies scampered back inside. Tired and happy after playing all day, they were soon fast asleep.

"I told you to wait till later," said Mrs. Rabbit. "Now try counting them."

So Mr. Rabbit began counting. "One, two, three, four, five, six, seven, eight, nine, TEN!" he cried. "I've done it!"

"Oh, no you haven't," said Mrs. Rabbit. . . .

"You still have to count the littlest ones!"